100 THINGS TO DO IN MONTGOMERY ALABAMA BEFORE YOU DIE

T0038581

ONE WAY